THE MICROWAVE LIBRARY

■ C O O K I N G   W I T H ■

Soups

AND HORS D'OEUVRES

ELIZABETH CORNISH

THE MICROWAVE LIBRARY

COOKING WITH

Soups

AND HORS D'OEUVRES

ELIZABETH CORNISH

NEW BURLINGTON BOOKS

THE
MICROWAVE
LIBRARY

A QUINTET BOOK

Published by New Burlington Books
6 Blundell Street
London N7 9BH

ISBN 1-85076-090-X

This book was designed and produced by
Quintet Publishing Limited
6 Blundell Street
London N7 9BH

Art Director: Peter Bridgewater
Photographers: Michael Bull and Trevor Wood
Home Economist: Veronica Bull
Typeset in Great Britain by
Central Southern Typesetters, Eastbourne
Manufactured in Hong Kong by Regent
Publishing Services Limited
Printed in Hong Kong by Leefung-Asco Printers
Limited

CONTENTS

SOUPS AND HORS D'OEUVRES

SOUPS and hors d'oeuvres can be prepared ahead of time for reheating, which in a microwave will not spoil either their good looks or taste. Some soups and starters can be assembled and cooked at the last minute, others can be eaten cold.

When you are cooking with a microwave, it is particularly easy to plan a menu as much to please the eye as the palate, because foods keep their natural shapes and colours. This is important when you are entertaining, as there is nothing more pleasing to guests than having something really appetizing placed before them, and nothing more pleasing to a host than an expression of delighted anticipation – and clean plates at the end of the meal.

When you're not entertaining, a soup or a starter, or a soup *and* a starter, can make a whole meal, especially when served with bread and salad.

Home-made soups, like home-made bread, are a simple luxury that until recently many cooks could not spare the time to make. With a microwave, you can enjoy the satisfying flavour and natural goodness of a soup made from fresh ingredients in only a little more time than it takes to heat up a tin, or reconstitute a packet.

There is a soup in this book to suit every occasion and taste, from delicate cool numbers for summer dinner parties to a thick fish soup that will leave you wanting only a siesta to follow.

As for starters – there is a wide and interesting range of appetizers both hot and cold, light and substantial, so that you will have several choices to complement your main course. For an elegant late-night supper you could opt simply to serve a selection of starters, with perhaps fruit and coffee to follow.

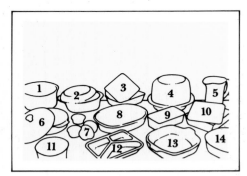

A selection of cookware, some of it specially designed for the microwave oven, which is suitable for microwaving.

1 Thorpak cake dish **2** Thorpak casserole dish **3** Microware freezer dishes **4** Roasting dish **5** Thorpak jug **6** Browning dish **7** Minidishes (ramekins) **8** Double microwave serving dish **9** Glass loaf pan **10** Glass casserole with lid **11** Cake or soufflé dish **12** Three-section vegetable dish **13** Browning dish **14** Glass ovenproof dish

ABOUT THE MICROWAVE OVEN

IF YOU are new to cooking with the microwave, the first thing to do is to read the instruction booklet supplied with your model. This will tell you all you need to know about how your cooker works and how to operate it.

Microwave cookers work by emitting concentrated infra red radiation that penetrates and therefore heats food much faster than conventional cookers. They consequently save considerably on cooking time.

The microwave is like any other kitchen appliance that makes life easier for the cook. Once you are used to it, which takes remarkably little time for such a sophisticated gadget, experience will tell you how long it will take to cook or reheat a given dish. If in doubt, always undercook – you can easily add on another minute or so.

To familiarize yourself with the cooker try baking a potato. Scrub the potato and prick the skin a few times with a fork. Lay it on a piece of absorbent kitchen paper and cook on full power for about 6 minutes for a 175 g/6 oz potato. Stop cooking half-way through to turn the potato over. A successfully baked potato will demonstrate how easy microwave cooking is.

Remember to stir or rearrange items during cooking or the food may not be evenly cooked, and

always cover a dish with a lid or cling film (plastic wrap) which you have pierced in two or three places with a knife to make vents through which the steam can escape.

Don't use anything metallic in the microwave, and this includes china decorated with silver or gold leaf. If you want to test if a dish is microwave-proof, put it in the oven next to a cup of water and cook on full for a minute. If the water is hot and the dish stays cool, it is safe to use. If the dish is hotter than the water, avoid using it.

Always prick the skins of vegetables and fish to prevent them from bursting. Eggs should always be pricked for the same reason. Never put an egg in its shell in the microwave – it will explode.

All the recipes in this book are timed for a 700-watt oven, and where the recipe times are not specific, this is to avoid errors. A microwave may be a scientific instrument, but even identical ovens may cook at slightly different rates, and neither cooks nor food can be standardized – no two carrots are the same shape and no two cooks cut them in the same way.

However, the following can be taken as a general guide for ovens with a different power rating from that of the model used in the book. For every minute of cooking time specified in these recipes, add 5 seconds for a 650-watt oven, 10 seconds for a 600-watt oven and 30 seconds for a 500-watt oven. But remember, it is *always* safer to undercook and test.

Crockery, cutlery (flatware, glassware and cookware such as this must NOT be used in a microwave oven.

1 Ceramics with metal decoration **2** Dishes with metal decoration and glazes containing metal **3** Cutlery (silverware or flatware) **4** Metal flan tin and disposable foil bakeware **5** Glassware with metal rim or bands **6** Metal pots and pans **7** Metal bakeware **8** Metal skewers or fondue forks

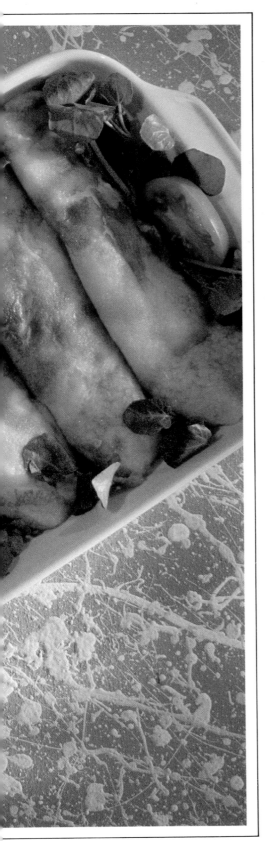

SPINACH AND RICOTTA PANCAKES

SERVES 4 / SET: FULL

Ingredients

1½ cups/175 g/6 oz plain (all-purpose) white flour

a pinch of salt

2 eggs

2 cups/450 ml/¾ pt milk

1 tbsp melted butter or oil

SPINACH AND RICOTTA FILLING

4 cups/1 kg/2 lb spinach

2 tbsp/25 g/1 oz butter

1¼ cups/250 g/8 oz ricotta cheese

salt and freshly ground black pepper

a pinch of nutmeg

Although pancakes can't themselves be made in the microwave, there is no better way of heating up stuffed pancakes so that each one tastes as if it had been freshly made and the edges aren't dry and leathery.

◆ First make the pancakes. Sift the flour with the salt into a bowl, make a well in the middle and break in the eggs. Add the milk slowly, beating to incorporate the flour.

◆ When half the milk has been added, stir in the melted butter or oil and beat until smooth. Add the remaining milk. The batter should be the consistency of thin cream. Leave it to stand for at least 30 minutes.

◆ For the filling, wash the spinach and discard any tough stalks and discoloured leaves.

◆ Put the butter in a large pot and cook for 1 minute until melted. Cram in the spinach, cover and cook for 6 minutes, turning the pot once, until the spinach is soft but still bright emerald green.

◆ Chop the spinach with the ricotta, mixing well, and season with salt, pepper and nutmeg.

◆ Make the pancakes on the hob. Pour a little oil into a heavy based pan and heat until very hot. Stir the batter well and spoon in enough to coat the bottom of the pan. Tilt and jiggle the pan over the heat until the pancake has set, then toss or turn it over with a spatula and cook the other side.

◆ Discard your first pancake as it will be too oily.

◆ Pile the pancakes on a plate as you make them, but don't attempt to keep them hot, or they will dry out.

◆ Divide the filling between the pancakes and roll up. Pack them into an oblong dish, cover with vented cling wrap (plastic wrap) and cook for 2–3 minutes until hot through.

◆ Serve with tomato sauce (see page 67).

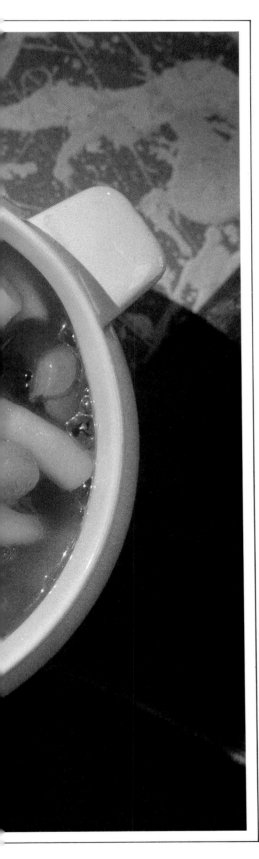

BORLOTTI BEAN SOUP

SERVES 4 / SET: FULL

Ingredients

2 cups/250 g/8 oz soup macaroni

oil

2 1/2 cups/600 ml/1 pt boiling meat stock

2 tbsp tomato pureé (paste)

2 cups/400 g/14 oz can borlotti beans, drained

salt and freshly ground black pepper

◆ Put the macaroni in a large pot with a little oil and pour over half the stock. Cover and cook for 8 minutes.
◆ Add the tomato purée (paste), diluted in the rest of the stock, and the borlotti beans, cover and cook for 4 minutes.
◆ Season to taste and serve, with grated cheese if liked.

Borlotti bean soup

MUSSEL AND POTATO SOUP

SERVES 4 / SET: FULL

Ingredients

7 cups/900 ml/1 1/2 pt mussels

45 ml/3 tbsp oil

1 small glass dry white wine

1 small onion, chopped

1 clove garlic, chopped

2 rashers (strips) bacon, chopped

2 1/2 cups/600 ml/1 pt boiling fish stock (see page 13)

2 cups/250 g/8 oz cooked potato, diced

1/3 cup/75 g/3 oz rice

salt and freshly ground black pepper

◆ Scrub the mussels thoroughly under cold running water and scrape away their beards. Discard any that are broken or damaged.
◆ Put half the oil in a large pot with the wine and cook for 2 minutes, until very hot. Add the mussels. Cover and cook for about 3 minutes, stirring halfway through, until the shells open. Discard any muscles that remain closed.
◆ Remove the mussels from their shells, keeping some shells for decoration. Put mussels and cooking liquor to one side.
◆ Put the remaining oil in the pot with the onion, garlic and bacon, cover and cook for 3 minutes. Add half the fish stock, stir in the cooked potato and rice. Cover and cook for 10 minutes, until the rice is tender.
◆ Stir in the remaining fish stock, add the mussels and their cooking liquor and season to taste.
◆ Serve, decorated with a couple of mussels in their shells if liked.

FISH SOUP

SERVES 4 / SET: FULL

Ingredients

1 tbsp olive oil
1 onion, chopped
1 clove garlic, crushed (minced)
½ fennel bulb, chopped
2 large or 4 small tomatoes, skinned and chopped
1 kg/2 lb mixed white fish, cleaned and skinned
15 g/2 tsp turmeric
2½ cups/600 ml/1 pt boiling water or fish stock (see below)
salt and freshly ground black pepper
Parmesan cheese

NOTE *To make a fish stock, put the fish trimmings and heads in a large pot, add a bay leaf, a piece each of carrot, celery and onion and pour over 2½ cups/600 ml/1 pt boiling water. Cover and cook in the microwave for 7 minutes, then strain off the stock.*

◆ Put the oil in a large pot and cook for 30 seconds. Stir in the onion, garlic and fennel, cover and cook for 5 minutes.

◆ Add the tomatoes and fish, stir in the turmeric, then pour over the water or stock. Cover and cook for 8–10 minutes, until the fish is done.

◆ Season to taste and serve with plenty of Parmesan cheese.

CHESTNUT SOUP

SERVES 4 / SET: FULL

Ingredients

2 tbsp/25 g/1 oz butter
1 large onion, chopped
1 carrot, chopped
1 stick (stack) celery, chopped
1¾ cups/400 g/14 oz can chestnut purée (paste)
3¾ cups/900 ml/1½ pt very hot milk and stock, mixed
salt and freshly ground black pepper

NOTE *If making this soup with fresh chestnuts, peel them according to the instructions in the recipe for Savoury Stuffed Vine Leaves (see page 27) and cook them in the stock and milk for 10–12 minutes until soft, then blend the soup in a liquidizer.*

◆ Put the butter in a large pot and cook for one minute until melted. Stir in the onion, carrot and celery. Cover and cook for 5 minutes.

◆ Stir in the chestnut purée and pour over the hot milk and stock. Cover and cook for 6 minutes.

◆ Season and serve.

Chestnut soup

MINESTRONE ALLA MILANESE

SERVES 6 / SET: FULL

Ingredients

4 rashers (strips) bacon
2 tbsp/25 g/1 oz butter
1 onion, chopped
1 clove garlic, chopped
1 carrot, chopped
1 stick (stack) celery, chopped
2 courgettes (zucchini), sliced
1/3 cup/75 g/3 oz rice
3³⁄4 cups/900 ml/1¹⁄2 pt boiling chicken stock
1/4 white cabbage, shredded
4 cups/500 g/1 lb peas
3/4 cup/200 g/7 oz can tomatoes, mashed, with juice
a small handful of parsley, chopped
a few leaves each of basil and sage
salt and freshly ground black pepper
Parmesan cheese

◆ Put the bacon on a plate or bacon rack covered with absorbent kitchen paper (paper towels) and microwave for 4 minutes, turning once. Cut into pieces and set aside.
◆ Put the butter in a large pot and cook for 1 minute until melted. Stir in the onion, garlic, carrot and celery, cover with vented cling wrap (plastic wrap) and cook for 4 minutes.
◆ Add the courgettes (zucchini) and rice, pour over half the stock, cover and cook for 10 minutes.
◆ Add the cabbage, peas, tomatoes and herbs, pour on the rest of the stock, cover and cook for 5 minutes.
◆ Season to taste and serve with Parmesan cheese.

PASTA AND PEA SOUP

SERVES 4 / SET: FULL

Ingredients
2 tbsp/25 g/1 oz butter
1 onion, chopped
1 clove garlic, crushed (minced)
1 stick (stack) celery, finely chopped
1 carrot, finely chopped
1 tbsp tomato purée (paste)
2½ cups/600 ml/1 pt boiling beef stock
1 cup/100 g/4 oz pasta shapes
1 cup/200 g/7 oz peas
salt and freshly ground black pepper
a handful of parsley, chopped (optional)
Parmesan cheese (optional)

◆ Put the butter in a large pot and cook for 1 minute until melted. Stir in the onion, garlic, celery and carrot. Cover with vented cling wrap (plastic wrap) and cook for 4 minutes.

◆ Stir in the tomato purée (paste), pour over the boiling stock and add the pasta. Cover and cook for 8 minutes.

◆ Add the peas 6 minutes before the end of cooking time if fresh, 4 minutes if canned or defrosted.

◆ Season to taste and serve sprinkled with parsley or Parmesan cheese if liked.

GARLIC MUSHROOMS

SERVES 4 / SET: FULL

Ingredients
16 mushrooms, about 3 cm/1½ in across
15 ml/1 tbsp oil
2 cloves garlic, crushed (minced)
60 ml/4 tbsp chopped fresh herbs
2 slices wholemeal (whole wheat) bread, soaked in milk and squeezed
salt and freshly ground black pepper

◆ Peel the mushrooms or wipe them. Cut off the stalks and chop finely.
◆ Put the oil in a small bowl and cook for 30 seconds. Add the garlic and cook for 1 minute.
◆ Mix the garlic with the mushroom stalks, herbs and bread, mashing it to a paste.
◆ Divide the filling between the mushroom caps, put them in a lightly oiled dish, covered with vented cling wrap (plastic wrap) and cook for 5 minutes, turning once.
◆ Serve hot.

CREAMED TOMATO SOUP

SERVES 4 / SET: FULL

Ingredients
2 kg/4 lb ripe tomatoes
1 onion
⅓ cup/50 g/2 oz chopped ham
½ cucumber, diced
5 ml/1 tsp Worcestershire sauce
a squeeze of lemon juice
⅔ cup/125 ml/5 fl oz carton cream
chopped basil or parsley

This is a luxurious soup to make if you have a glut of fresh tomatoes. The finished soup will be lukewarm — the ideal temperature at which to serve it.

◆ Plunge the tomatoes into boiling water for 1 minute until the skins split. Peel them and chop them, discarding the seeds and the cores.
◆ Put them in a large pot, cover with vented cling wrap (plastic wrap) and cook for 5 minutes, stirring once, until thick and pulpy. Blend in the liquidizer until smooth.
◆ Put the onion in a cloth (cheesecloth) and squeeze it hard over the tomatoes to get as much juice out as you can.
◆ Stir all the ingredients together in a large bowl and serve, sprinkled with basil or parsley.

Creamed tomato soup

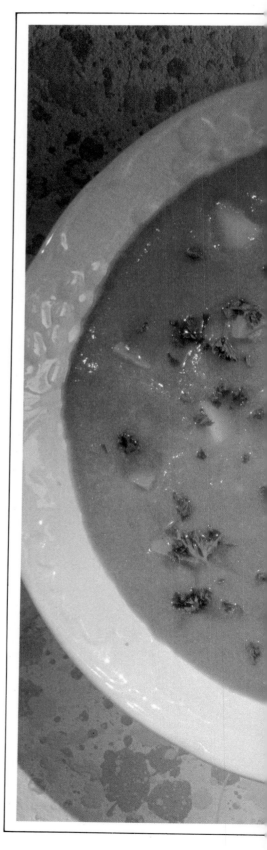

CHICKEN LIVER AND BACON ROLLS

SERVES 4 / SET: FULL

Ingredients

½ cup/100 g/4 oz chicken livers
60 ml/4 tbsp dry sherry
15 ml/1 tbsp mushroom ketchup
1 clove garlic, crushed (minced)
8 rashers (strips) bacon

These can also make tasty little snacks to serve at a drinks party.

◆ Put the livers in a bowl and sprinkle over the sherry and mushroom ketchup. Stir in the garlic and leave to marinate for an hour, stirring occasionally.

◆ Lay the bacon on a paper towel on a bacon rack or plate and cook for 4 minutes.

◆ Cut the rashers (strips) in half, divide the chicken livers between them, roll up and secure with wooden cocktail sticks or toothpicks.

◆ Put the bacon rolls back on the rack and cook for 5 minutes, turning once.

◆ Serve hot.

SOUSED HERRING

SERVES 4 / SET: FULL

Ingredients

4 herrings, filleted
salt and freshly ground black pepper
2/3 cup/150 ml/1/4 pt cider vinegar
2/3 cup/150 ml/1/4 pt water
2 1/2 ml/1/2 tsp pickling spice
1 bayleaf
1 large cooking apple, peeled and sliced
1 onion, sliced

◆ Roll up the fillets and secure with cocktail sticks or toothpicks.
◆ Season the fish and place in a shallow dish with the vinegar, water, pickling spice and bayleaf. Top with apple and onion.
◆ Cover with vented cling wrap (plastic wrap) and cook for 8 minutes, turning once. Allow to cool
◆ Chill and remove with a slotted spoon to serve on a bed of lettuce leaves. Garnish with the apple and onion.

Soused herring

PRAWN (SHRIMP) STUFFED TOMATOES

S E R V E S   4 / S E T :   F U L L

Ingredients

4 large beef tomatoes
salt
2 tbsp/25 g/1 oz butter
1 onion, finely chopped
1 clove garlic, finely chopped
1 generous cup/150 g/6 oz peeled prawns (shrimp)
75 g/3 oz fresh white breadcrumbs
30 ml/2 tbsp chopped parsley
30 ml/2 tbsp tomato purée (paste)
cayenne pepper
lemon wedges

◆ Cut the tops off the tomatoes, scoop out the pulp and reserve. Sprinkle the insides of the tomatoes with salt and leave upside down to drain.

◆ Meanwhile, make the filling. Put the butter in a bowl and cook for 1 minute. Stir in onion and garlic. Cover with vented cling wrap (plastic wrap) and cook for 2 minutes.

◆ Stir in tomato pulp and remaining ingredients, except lemon wedges. Mix well and season with cayenne pepper to taste.

◆ Stuff the tomatoes and put them upright in a dish they just fit. Cook, covered with vented cling wrap (plastic wrap), for 5 minutes, then allow to stand for 1–2 minutes.

◆ Serve hot with lemon wedges.

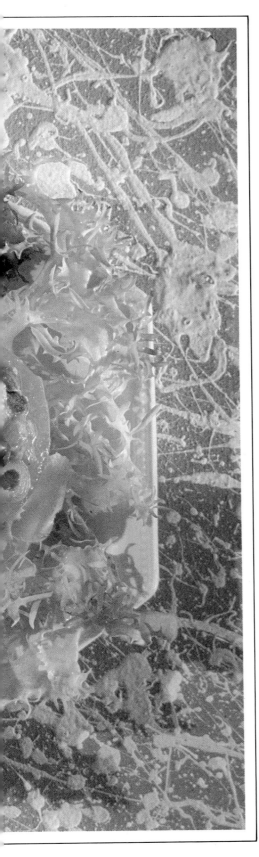

Anchovy-stuffed tomatoes

ANCHOVY-STUFFED TOMATOES

S E R V E S   4   /   S E T :   F U L L

Ingredients

4 large beef tomatoes

salt

2 tbsp/25 g/1 oz butter

1 onion, chopped

8 anchovy fillets, soaked in water and drained

1 bunch of parsley, chopped

approx. 30 capers

30 ml/2 tbsp breadcrumbs

10 olives, stoned (pitted) and chopped

freshly ground black pepper

◆ Cut the tops off the tomatoes, scoop out the pulp and reserve. Sprinkle the insides of the tomatoes with salt and leave upside down to drain.

◆ Meanwhile, make the filling. Put the butter in a bowl and cook for 1 minute until melted. Stir in the onion and cook for 2 minutes.

◆ Pound the anchovy fillets and stir into the onion with the remaining ingredients. Season with pepper, and salt if necessary. (The salt in the anchovies may be enough, so make sure you taste the mixture first.) Fill the tomatoes with the mixture.

◆ Put the tomatoes upright in a dish they just fit and cook, covered with vented cling wrap (plastic wrap), for 5 minutes.

◆ Allow to stand for 1–2 minutes and serve hot.

SAVOURY STUFFED VINE LEAVES

S E R V E S   4   /   S E T :   F U L L

Ingredients

1 generous cup/250 g/8 oz chestnuts

olive oil

1 small onion, chopped

2 cloves garlic, crushed (minced)

1 cup/250 g/8 oz brown rice

2½ cups/600 ml/1 pt boiling water

1 tbsp/15 g/½ oz butter

2 cups/100 g/4 oz mushrooms, chopped

2 tomatoes, peeled and chopped

30 ml/2 tbsp chopped fresh mixed herbs

salt and freshly ground black pepper

20 vine leaves

◆ To prepare chestnuts, pierce the skins with a sharp knife and heat them in the microwave in 3 batches for 1½ minutes per batch. Peel off the skins.

◆ Put 15 ml/1 tbsp oil in a large pot and cook for 30 seconds. Add the onion and garlic, cover with vented cling wrap (plastic wrap) and cook for 2 minutes.

◆ Stir in the rice and pour on the boiling water. Cover with vented cling wrap (plastic wrap) and cook for 12 minutes. Drop in the chestnuts and cook for a further 10 minutes. Let the pot stand for 5–10 minutes.

◆ Put the butter in a dish and cook for 1 minute until melted. Add the mushrooms, tomatoes and herbs and sprinkle with pepper. Stir to coat in the butter, cover with vented cling wrap (plastic wrap) and cook for 3 minutes.

◆ Chop the chestnuts and mix them into the rice with the mushrooms and tomatoes. Place a spoonful of the stuffing on each vine leaf, roll them up and pack them, join down, into an oblong dish.

◆ Brush the tops of the vine leaves with olive oil and cook for 1½ minutes.

◆ Serve hot.

ARTICHOKES WITH MELTED BUTTER

SERVES 4 / SET: FULL

Ingredients

4 artichokes

lemon juice

⅔ cup/150 ml/¼ pt boiling water

½ cup/100 g/4 oz butter, diced

◆ Soak the artichokes for an hour in a bowl of water acidulated with a little lemon juice to clean them of earth and insects.

◆ Trim away the tough outer leaves and cut the stalks off neatly so that the artichokes stand up on their bases. Rub any cut edges with lemon juice to stop them discolouring. There is no need to cut the points off the leaves – this only spoils the look of the vegetable.

◆ Put the artichokes in a large pot with the boiling water and cook, covered, for 15–20 minutes, rearranging the artichokes twice.

◆ To test if they are done, tug gently at one of the lower leaves on the largest artichoke. If it will come away easily, they are ready. Drain the artichokes upside down in a colander.

◆ Put the butter in a small jug and cook for 1½ minutes until melted.

◆ Stand the artichokes on individual plates and pass the butter round. Provide your guests with finger bowls and generous napkins.

GARLIC PRAWNS (SHRIMP) WITH EGGS

SERVES 4 / SET: FULL AND MEDIUM

Ingredients

30 ml/2 tbsp olive oil

1 fat clove garlic, crushed (minced)

1½ cups/250 g/8 oz shelled prawns (shrimp)

4 eggs

A starter with a distinctively Spanish flavour.

◆ Divide the oil equally between 4 individual ramekin dishes and then the garlic. Cover with vented cling wrap and cook on full power for 1 minute.

◆ Divide the prawns (shrimp) between the dishes and stir to coat in the oil. Push the prawns to one side of the dish and break an egg into the other.

◆ Pierce each yolk carefully with a cocktail stick (toothpick) to prevent them bursting, cover the dishes with vented cling wrap (plastic wrap) and cook on medium power for 3½ minutes, turning the dishes once.

◆ Let the dishes rest for 1 minute, then serve with crusty bread to mop up the garlic juices.

Garlic prawns (shrimp) with eggs

CHEESE AND ONION SOUP

SERVES 4 / SET: FULL

Ingredients

3 tbsp/40 g/1 1/2 oz butter
2 medium onions, sliced
2 tbsp plain (all-purpose) flour
2 1/2 cups/600 ml/1 pt boiling chicken stock
1 1/2 cups/175 g/6 oz strong Cheddar cheese, finely grated
salt
Worcestershire sauce

A very tasty and nourishing thick soup to serve with wholemeal (whole wheat) bread on a cold winter's day.

◆ Put the butter in a large pot and cook for 1 minute until melted. Add the onions, stirring to coat, cover and cook for 4 minutes. Stir in the flour and cook for 1 minute. Stir again.

◆ Pour on the stock and cook for 5 minutes, stirring every minute, until thickened.

◆ Stir in the cheese, a little at a time, until it has melted. Season with salt and Worcestershire sauce.

◆ Return to the microwave for a further 1 1/2 minutes to reheat, then serve.

PIPERADE

SERVES 2—4
SET: FULL AND DEFROST

Ingredients

30 ml/2 tbsp olive oil

½ Spanish onion, finely sliced

1 clove garlic, chopped

½ green pepper, cut into julienne strips

½ red pepper, cut into julienne strips

1 large tomato, peeled and finely sliced

5 eggs

15 ml/1 tbsp chopped fresh basil

salt and freshly ground black pepper

sprigs of watercress

This makes an interesting first course before plainly cooked fish or meat, rather like the French might eat an omelette (omelet) before a steak.

◆ Pour olive oil into a shallow oval dish and cook for 1 minute. Stir in onion, garlic and peppers and cook for 3 minutes. Add the tomatoes and cook for a further 2 minutes, or until vegetables are done.

◆ Beat the eggs with the chopped basil and season. Stir egg mixture into vegetables. Cook for about 3 minutes on defrost power, or until nearly cooked, stirring every minute to scramble the eggs.

◆ Allow to stand for 1 minute, then garnish with watercress and serve.

Piperade

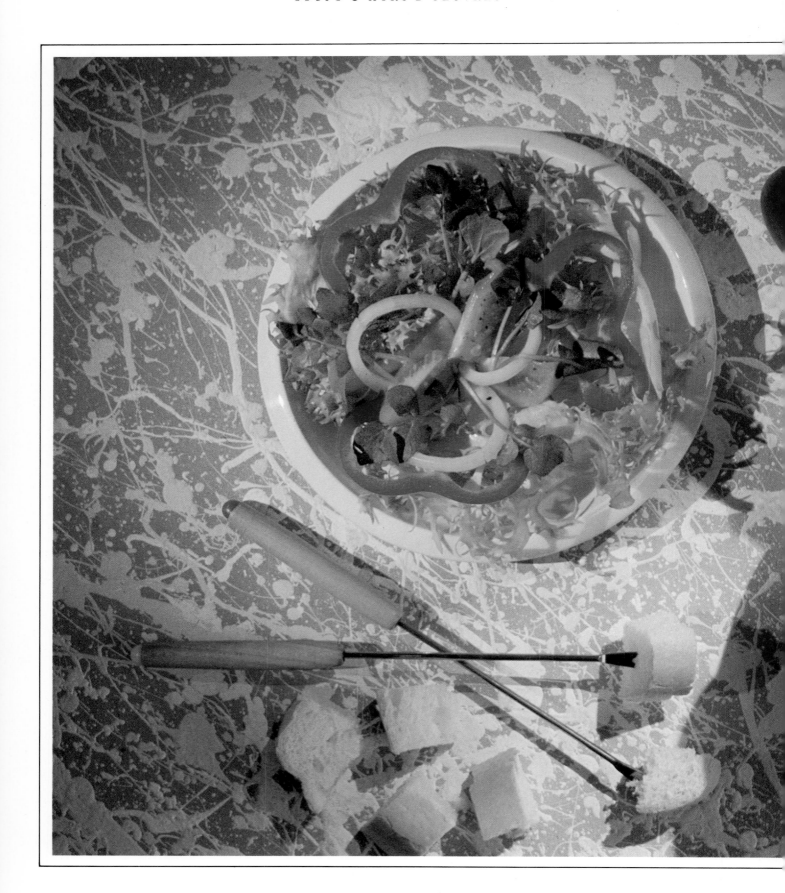

CHEESE FONDUE

SERVES 4 / SET: FULL

Ingredients

1 clove garlic, finely chopped
¾ cup/200 ml/⅓ pt dry white wine
2 cups/225 g/8 oz Gruyère cheese, finely grated
5 g/2 tsp cornflour (cornstarch)
30 ml/2 tbsp brandy
freshly ground black pepper
nutmeg

◆ Put garlic and wine in a bowl and cook for 2 minutes.

◆ Add cheese. Cook for 4 minutes, stirring 3 times, until cheese has melted.

◆ Mix together cornflour (cornstarch), brandy, pepper and nutmeg. Stir into cheese. Cook for 4 minutes.

◆ Serve with French bread cut into bite-sized pieces and accompany with a crisp salad. Provide each guest with a fondue fork or kebab (kebob) stick for spearing the bread.

WELSH RAREBIT

SERVES 4
SET: FULL AND MEDIUM

Ingredients

4 slices wholemeal (whole wheat) toast
4 slices ham
2 cups/225 g/8 oz grated Cheddar cheese
1 tbsp/15 g/½ oz butter
salt and freshly ground black pepper
2½ ml/½ tsp Worcestershire sauce
2½ ml/½ tsp paprika
45 ml/3 tbsp single (cereal) cream
tomato wedges
sprigs of watercress

This can also be served instead of a dessert, if you prefer to end your meal on a savoury note.

◆ Top each slice of toast with a slice of ham and keep warm.
◆ Put the cheese and butter in a bowl and cook on full, stirring every minute, for 3 minutes until cheese has melted.
◆ Season, stir in the Worcestershire sauce, paprika and cream and cook on medium for 8 minutes, stirring every minute, until smooth and creamy.
◆ Top the toast and ham with the cheese mixture and serve garnished with tomato wedges and sprigs of watercress.

Welsh rarebit

CHICK PEA (GARBANZO) SOUP

SERVES 4 / SET: FULL

Ingredients

2 tbsp/25 g/1 oz butter
1 small onion, chopped
1 clove garlic, chopped
¾ cup/200 g/7 oz can tomatoes, mashed, with juice
2 cups/400 g/14 oz can chick peas (garbanzos), drained
a pinch of marjoram, or 5 ml/1 tsp chopped fresh marjoram
2½ cups/600 ml/1 pt boiling beef stock
salt and freshly ground black pepper
4 slices crusty white bread, toasted
Parmesan cheese

If using dried chick peas (garbanzos), soak them overnight, drain and boil vigorously in fresh water on the hob for 10 minutes. Turn down the heat and simmer until cooked. This may take up to 5 hours, depending on the age of the chick peas. How much simpler and cheaper to use the canned variety!

◆ Put the butter in a large pot and cook for 1 minute, until melted. Add the onion and garlic, cover and cook for 2 minutes.
◆ Add the tomatoes, chick peas and marjoram. Pour on the beef stock, cover and cook for 6 minutes. Season to taste.
◆ Lay a slice of toasted bread in each of 4 soup plates. Pour over the hot soup and serve with Parmesan cheese.

VEGETABLE SOUP WITH PESTO

SERVES 4 / SET: FULL

Ingredients

1 cup/250 g/8 oz spinach
3 tbsp/40 g/1½ oz butter
2 cooked potatoes, diced
1 cup/100 g/4 oz green beans, cut into pieces
½ white cabbage, shredded
1 leek, sliced
1 onion, sliced
2½ cups/600 ml/1 pt boiling chicken stock
PESTO
4 cloves garlic
4 tbsp grated Parmesan cheese
2 tbsp pine nuts
a large bunch of basil
30–60 ml/2–4 tbsp olive oil

Stir a tablespoonful of pesto sauce into a tureen of soup for a lovely garlicky flavour. Make up a small jar of the sauce and keep it in the fridge for use on pasta too.

◆ First make the pesto by blending together all the ingredients, except the oil, in a liquidizer or pounding them in a mortar with a pestle.

◆ Add enough olive oil to make a thick, smooth paste. Store the sauce in a jar in the fridge and use as required.

◆ For the soup, wash the spinach and discard any tough stalks and discoloured leaves. Cram it into a big pot with half the butter, cover with vented cling wrap (plastic wrap) and cook for 6 minutes, turning once, until soft. Chop finely and set aside.

◆ Put the rest of the butter in the pot and cook for 30 seconds until melted. Add the remaining vegetables, stirring to coat them with the butter. Cover with vented cling wrap (plastic wrap) and cook for 5 minutes.

◆ Pour over the chicken stock, stir in the spinach and cook for a further 6 minutes, stirring twice.

◆ Stir in a tablespoonful of pesto sauce and serve. Offer salt and pepper at the table.

MOULES A LA MARINIERE

SERVES 2 / SET: FULL

Ingredients

10 cups/1.25 l/2 pt mussels
4 tbsp/50 g/2 oz butter
1 onion, chopped
1 clove garlic, chopped
a handful of fresh parsley, chopped
freshly ground black pepper
1 glass dry white wine

◆ Scrub the mussels thoroughly under cold running water, scraping away beards. Discard mussels that are open or broken.

◆ Put the butter in a large bowl and cook for 1 minute. Add the onion, garlic, parsley, pepper and wine. Cover and cook for 2 minutes.

◆ Add the musels, cover and cook for about 3 minutes until shells are open, giving the dish a good stir halfway through. Discard any mussels that remain closed.

◆ Serve in deep soup plates with French bread to mop up the juices and provide a dish for the discarded shells.

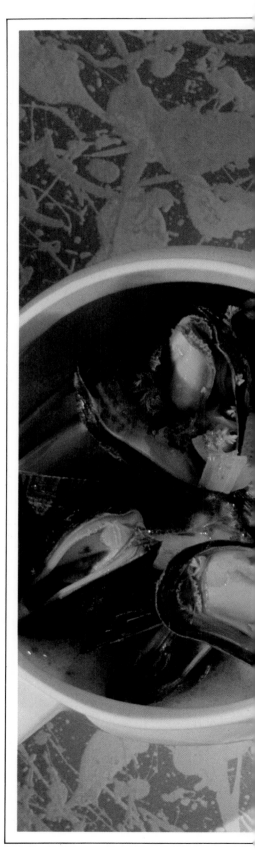

Moules à la marinière

SMOKED SALMON SCRAMBLED EGGS

SERVES 2 / SET: FULL

Ingredients

6 medium eggs
15 ml/1 tbsp milk
freshly ground black pepper
²/₃ cup/100 g/4 oz smoked salmon, cut into 1-cm/½-in squares
2 tbsp/25 g/1 oz butter
a pinch of cayenne pepper

This most luxurious starter makes a good prelude to a main dish of vegetables. Serve it with chilled Champagne or Buck's Fizz. Have thin triangles of wholemeal (whole wheat) toast buttered and kept hot on warmed plates so that all that remains to be done once the eggs are cooked is to pop the cork.

◆ Beat the eggs with the milk and season with black pepper. Stir in the salmon.

◆ Put the butter in a shallow oval dish and cook for 1 minute until melted.

◆ Stir in the eggs and smoked salmon. Cook for about 3 minutes, or until nearly done, stirring every minute.

◆ When the eggs are thick and creamy, pile them onto the hot toast. Add a sprinkling of cayenne pepper, allow to stand for 1 minute, then serve.

RISOTTO

S E R V E S   4 / S E T :   F U L L

Ingredients

½ cup/100 g/4 oz butter
1 large onion, chopped
2 small courgettes (zucchini), diced
1 carrot, diced
1 large tomato, peeled and chopped
1 cup/50 g/2 oz mushrooms, wiped and sliced
1¾ cups/400 g/14 oz long-grain rice
4½ cups/750 ml/1¾ pt boiling chicken stock
15 ml/1 tbsp tomato purée (paste)
salt and freshly ground black pepper
Parmesan cheese

This makes a substantial starter when there is plainly cooked meat or fish to follow. A risotto should be moist and succulent, not dry and fluffy.

◆ Put half the butter in a large bowl and cook for 1 minute. Stir in the vegetables, cover and cook for 8 minutes, stirring once.

◆ Stir in the rice, pour over the stock and add the tomato purée (paste). Season with a little salt, cover and cook for 15 minutes, stirring once.

◆ Allow to stand, covered, for 7 minutes. Stir in the remaining butter, plenty of black pepper and some Parmesan cheese.

◆ Serve, with more Parmesan cheese separately.

Risotto

KIPPER PATE

SERVES 4 / SET: MEDIUM

Ingredients

4 frozen kipper fillets
1 onion, finely chopped
2 tbsp/25 g/1 oz butter
15 ml/1 tbsp lemon juice
6 tbsp/75 g/3 oz full fat cream cheese
15 ml/1 tbsp sherry
salt and freshly ground black pepper
parsley
lemon twists

◆ Put the kippers, onion, butter and lemon juice in a dish, cover and cook on medium for 8–10 minutes, turning once.
◆ Purée the kippers and onions with the sherry and cream cheese in a blender, or mash with a fork, and season to taste.
◆ Fill 4 individual ramekin dishes with the pâté and garnish with sprigs of parsley and lemon twists.
◆ Chill and serve with hot toast.

Chicken liver pâté

CHICKEN LIVER PATE

SERVES 4 / SET: FULL

Ingredients

1 cup/225 g/8 oz chicken livers
1 small onion, finely chopped
2 cloves garlic, crushed (minced)
⅔ cup/150 g/5 oz butter
the leaves from 2 sprigs of fresh thyme, chopped
15 ml/1 tbsp port
15 ml/1 tbsp cream
salt and freshly ground black pepper
sprigs of fresh thyme
juniper berries

◆ Put the livers, onion, garlic, half the butter and the thyme in a bowl. Cover with vented cling wrap (plastic wrap) and cook for 5 minutes, stirring once.

◆ Put the mixture in a liquidizer, with the port and cream and blend until smooth. Season and divide between 4 individual ramekin dishes.

◆ Put the remaining butter in a bowl and cook for 30 seconds, or until melted. Pour over the pâté and chill.

◆ Garnish with fresh thyme and juniper berries and serve with crusty bread or triangles of wholemeal (whole wheat) toast.

THICK TOMATO SOUP

SERVES 4 / SET: FULL

Ingredients

30 ml/2 tbsp olive oil
1 or 2 cloves garlic, crushed (minced)
1 kg/2 lb ripe tomatoes, skinned and chopped
2½ cups/600 ml/1 pt boiling meat stock
salt and freshly ground black pepper
4 slices stale crusty white bread
a few leaves of sage and basil, chopped

This is a favourite supper time soup with children in Italy.

◆ Put the olive oil in a large pot and cook for 2 minutes. Add the garlic, stirring well to coat. Cook for 1 minute. Stir in the tomatoes, cover and cook for 8 minutes, stirring once or twice.

◆ Pour on the meat stock, stir well and cook for a further 3 minutes. Season to taste.

◆ Lay a slice of bread in each of 4 soup plates. Pour the soup over and sprinkle sage and basil leaves on top.

◆ Serve with grated cheese if liked.

CABBAGE SOUP

SERVES 4 / SET: FULL

Ingredients
1 savoy cabbage
2½ cups/600 ml/1 pt boiling chicken stock
salt and freshly ground black pepper
4 slices crusty white bread
Parmesan cheese

◆ Wash the cabbage, discard any discoloured or tough leaves, quarter it and cut out the stalk.

◆ Put the leaves in a roasting or boiling bag with a generous spoonful of water and tie the top loosely. Microwave for 6 minutes. Remove and chop the cabbage.

◆ Put the cabbage in a large pot, pour over the boiling stock and cook, covered, for 3 minutes. Season to taste.

◆ Lay a slice of bread in the bottom of each of 4 soup plates. Pour over the soup and serve with plenty of Parmesan cheese.

MUSHROOM SOUP

SERVES 4 / SET: FULL

Ingredients

3 tbsp/40 g/1½ oz butter

1 small onion, chopped

1 clove garlic

12 cups/750 g/1½ lb mushrooms, peeled or wiped, and sliced

2½ cups/600 ml/1 pt boiling chicken stock

⅓ cup/100 g/4 oz tomatoes, peeled and chopped

salt and freshly ground black pepper

a pinch of nutmeg

◆ Put the butter in a large pot and cook for 1 minute. Add the onion and garlic, whole, cover with vented cling wrap (plastic wrap) and cook for 1 minute.

◆ Stir in the mushrooms, add a few spoonfuls of the chicken stock, cover and cook for 4 minutes, stirring once.

◆ Remove the garlic, add the tomatoes and pour on the rest of the chicken stock. Cover and cook for 4 minutes.

◆ Season to taste, add the nutmeg and serve.

BROAD (LIMA) BEAN AND HAM SOUP

SERVES 4 / SET: FULL

Ingredients

2 tbsp/25 g/1 oz butter
1 onion, chopped
1 clove garlic, crushed
1/3 cup/50 g/2 oz diced ham, off the bone
1.25 kg/2 1/2 lb broad (lima) beans
(2 cups/500 g/1 lb beans shelled weight)
5 cups/1 1/2 pt boiling chicken stock
salt and freshly ground black pepper
30 ml/2 tbsp cream

This soup is best made with the first young broad (lima) beans of the season. Later in the summer, as the beans get tougher, remove the inner skins by lifting the beans from the soup with a slotted ladle when they are cooked, and pressing them out of the skins between your thumb and forefinger. Out of season, use canned or frozen beans.

◆ Put the butter in a large pot and cook for 1 minute until melted. Stir in the onion and garlic and cook, covered, for 2 minutes.
◆ Add the ham and beans and pour over the stock. Cover and cook for 6 minutes, or until the beans are tender. Season to taste.
◆ Pour into soup plates and add a swirl of cream.

Broad (lima) bean and ham soup

CURRIED PARSNIP SOUP

SERVES 4 / SET: FULL

Ingredients

1 tbsp/15 g/½ oz butter

2½ ml/½ tsp fennel seeds

1 slice fresh root ginger

1 very large parsnip, finely sliced, weighing about 500 g/1¼ lb

1¼ cups/300 ml/½ pt boiling chicken stock

1¼ cups/300 ml/½ pt hot milk (approx.)

salt and freshly ground black pepper

a pinch of garam masala

The curry spices bring out the delicious natural sweetness of the parsnip. Parsnips are even sweeter after the first frost, which causes their sugar content to rise.

◆ Put the butter in a pot and cook for 1 minute until very hot. Add the fennel seeds and ginger, cover and cook for 45 seconds. Add the parsnip and 1–2 tbsp water.

◆ Cover and cook for 8 minutes, turning once, until the parsnip is really tender.

◆ Add the boiling chicken stock and cook for 3 minutes. Remove the ginger and blend the soup in a liquidizer.

◆ Add enough hot milk to reach the desired consistency, season to taste with salt and pepper and stir in a pinch of garam masala.

◆ Heat through in the microwave for a couple of minutes if necessary and serve.

YOUNG LEEKS WITH HOLLANDAISE SAUCE

SERVES 4 / SET: FULL AND MEDIUM OR DEFROST

Ingredients

500 g/1 lb young leeks
45 ml/3 tbsp water
HOLLANDAISE SAUCE
½ cup/100 g/4 oz butter, diced
30 ml/2 tbsp lemon juice
3 egg yolks
salt and white pepper

◆ Trim the leeks, slit them and wash thoroughly. Lay them in a dish, add the water, cover and cook on full power for 6–8 minutes, rearranging once, until tender.

◆ Let the dish stand for a few minutes, then drain and arrange the leeks on a heated serving dish or individual plates.

◆ Meanwhile, make the sauce. Put the butter in a bowl and cook for 2 minutes on medium or defrost until melted. Add the lemon juice and the egg yolks and whisk lightly.

◆ Cook on medium or defrost for 1 minute, whisk again and season with salt and white pepper (black pepper would spoil the appearance of the sauce).

◆ Transfer the sauce to a heated jug and serve with the leeks.

STUFFED COURGETTES (ZUCCHINI)

*SERVES 4
SET: FULL AND DEFROST*

Ingredients

15 ml/1 tbsp oil
1 small onion, chopped
1 clove of garlic, chopped
30 ml/2 tbsp chopped parsley
30 ml/2 tbsp grated Parmesan cheese
2 slices of bread, soaked in milk, squeezed out and crumbled
salt and freshly ground black pepper
4 fat courgettes (zucchini)
⅔ cup/150 ml/¼ pt Tomato Sauce (see page 67)

◆ Put the oil in a small bowl and cook for 30 seconds. Stir in the onion and garlic, cover with vented cling wrap (plastic wrap) and cook for 2 minutes.

◆ Mix in the parsley, Parmesan cheese and crumbled bread and season to taste.

◆ Cut the ends off the courgettes (zucchini) and hollow out the centres with an apple corer. Stuff the courgettes with the onion and bread mixture and arrange them in an oblong dish.

◆ Cover with vented cling wrap (plastic wrap) and cook on defrost power for 6 minutes, until tender, rearranging once.

◆ Serve the courgettes with hot tomato sauce (see page 67).

Young leeks with hollandaise sauce

COUNTRY PATE

SERVES 6—8 / SET: FULL

Ingredients

½ cup/100 g/4 oz butter
2 onions, chopped
2 cloves garlic, chopped
1¼ cups/300 g/10 oz pigs' liver, chopped
1⅔ cups/300 g/10 oz belly pork, trimmed and chopped
15 ml/1 tbsp chopped fresh sage leaves
60 ml/4 tbsp sherry
60 ml/4 tbsp double (heavy) cream
salt and freshly ground black pepper
bay leaves
juniper berries

◆ Put half the butter in a large bowl and cook for 1 minute. Stir in the onion and garlic, cover with vented cling wrap (plastic wrap) and cook for 4 minutes, until soft.

◆ Stir in the pigs' liver and belly pork, cover and cook for 8—10 minutes, stirring once or twice, until cooked through.

◆ Put the mixture in a liquidizer with the sage, sherry, cream and seasoning and blend until smooth. Fill a terrine with the pâté and smooth over the top.

◆ Dice the remaining butter and put it in a bowl and cook for 4 minutes until melted but not brown. Strain through a piece of muslin (cheese-cloth) and pour over the top of the pâté. Decorate with bay leaves and juniper berries and chill.

◆ Serve with hot toast.

HOT PASTA AND EGG SALAD

SERVES 4 / SET: FULL

Ingredients

2 cups/250 g/8 oz pasta shells
1¼ cups/300 ml/½ pt boiling water
30 ml/2 tbsp olive oil
⅓ cup/100 g/4 oz cooked or canned green beans
1 red pepper, cut into julienne strips
50 g/2 oz black olives
2 hardboiled (hard-cooked) eggs, quartered
salt and freshly ground black pepper

◆ Put the pasta shells in a pot with the boiling water, a little salt and a few drops of the oil. Cover and cook for 10 minutes.

◆ Leave to stand for 3 minutes, then drain and toss in the remaining oil.

◆ Mix in the beans, pepper and olives, season and divide the mixture between 4 individual dishes. Arrange the eggs on top.

◆ Serve and eat while the pasta is still warm – it makes an interesting contrast with the cold salad.

Hot pasta and egg salad

LENTIL SOUP

SERVES 4 / SET: FULL

Ingredients

2 tbsp/25 g/1 oz butter
a squeeze of lemon juice
1 onion, finely sliced
1 clove garlic, crushed (minced)
1/2 fresh green chilli (chili), minced
1 carrot, chopped
1 stick (stack) celery, finely sliced
2/3 cup/175 g/6 oz lentils
2 1/2 cups/600 ml/1 pt boiling chicken stock
salt and freshly ground black pepper
a handful of fresh parsley, roughly chopped

Brown and green lentils should be soaked overnight before use. The small red lentils can be used immediately.

◆ Put the butter in a large pot and cook for 1 minute until melted. Add the lemon juice, onion, garlic, chilli (chili), carrot and celery, cover with vented cling wrap (plastic wrap) and cook for 3 minutes.

◆ Stir in the lentils and pour over the boiling stock. Cover with vented cling wrap (plastic wrap) and cook until the lentils are soft: 15 minutes if using red lentils and 20 minutes if using green or brown.

◆ Blend half the soup, return to the pot and season to taste.

◆ Serve strewn with parsley.

CORN ON THE COB WITH HERB BUTTER

SERVES 4 / SET: FULL

Ingredients

1/2 cup/100 g/4 oz butter
4 corn on the cob, fresh or frozen
45 ml/3 tbsp chopped mixed fresh herbs

The herb butter can be made in advance, allowed to cool, then chilled and served in pats if required.

◆ Cut up the butter and place in a small dish. Cook for 1 minute.

◆ Brush the corn with some of the melted butter and wrap individually in waxed paper. Pack into a shallow dish.

◆ Cover and cook until grains are tender when pierced: 10 minutes if fresh or 12 if frozen.

◆ Transfer corn to serving dishes.

◆ Stir herbs into remaining butter and cook for 30 seconds.

◆ Pour herb butter over corn to serve.

Corn on the cob with herb butter

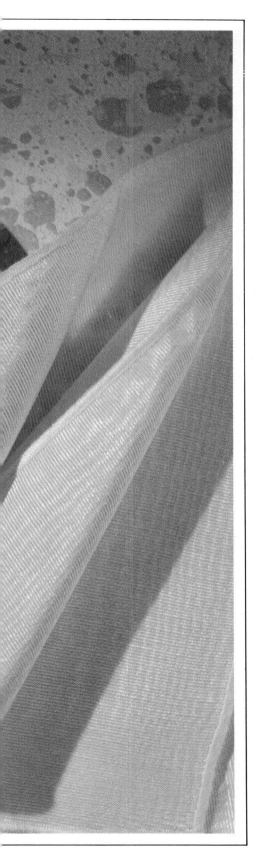

TOMATO, CARROT AND ORANGE SOUP

SERVES 4 / SET: FULL

Ingredients

3 cups/2 × 400 g/14 oz cans tomatoes, mashed, with juice
2 cups/225 g/8 oz carrots, chopped
juice of 1 orange
1 bayleaf
2½ cups/600 ml/1 pt hot chicken stock
rind of half an orange, finely grated
salt and freshly ground black pepper
single (cereal) cream

Carrots cook more quickly and evenly if they are chopped or chipped than they do when thickly sliced.

◆ Put tomatoes, carrots, orange juice and bayleaf in a bowl. Cover with vented cling wrap (plastic wrap) and cook for 10–15 minutes, stirring once or twice, until carrots are cooked.
◆ Remove the bayleaf and blend the mixture in a liquidizer. Return to the bowl and add the stock and orange rind. Season to taste.
◆ Cook for 4 minutes and serve hot or cold with a swirl of cream.

VARIATION You can make this soup with lemon instead of orange, using the juice of only half the fruit.

RICE AND TURNIP SOUP

SERVES 4 / SET: FULL

Ingredients

2 tbsp/25 g/1 oz butter
1 onion, chopped
2 turnips, peeled and diced
⅓ cup/75 g/3 oz rice
2½ cups/600 ml/1 pt boiling chicken stock
⅓ cup/50 g/2 oz ham, chopped
salt and freshly ground black pepper
a handful of parsley, chopped
Parmesan cheese

◆ Put the butter in a large pot and cook for 1 minute until melted. Stir in the onion and cook for 2 minutes.
◆ Stir in the turnips and rice, pour over enough chicken stock to cover, add the ham and cook, covered, for 12 minutes.
◆ Add the rest of the chicken stock, season to taste and add the parsley.
◆ Serve with plenty of Parmesan cheese.

Tomato, carrot and orange soup

CHERRY SOUP

SERVES 4 / SET: FULL

Ingredients

approx. 8 cups/1 kg/2 lb ripe black cherries
juice of half a lemon
ground cinnamon
honey to taste
water
soured (sour) cream
mint leaves (optional)

This is a lovely fruit soup from Hungary, where it might be eaten to sharpen the palate before a rich main course of duck or game. Serve it with black bread if you have a hearty appetite.

◆ Wash and pick over the cherries. Take out the stones. Put the cherries in a bowl with the lemon juice, cover with vented cling wrap (plastic wrap) and cook for 3–5 minutes until the fruit is very soft.

◆ Transfer the cherries to a liquidizer and blend with a little honey and a small pinch of cinnamon to taste. Add enough water to thin the soup to the desired consistency.

◆ Allow to cool, then chill in the fridge.

◆ Serve with a swirl of soured (sour) cream and decorate with mint leaves if liked.

TUSCAN VEGETABLE SOUP

SERVES 4 / SET: FULL

Ingredients

2 tbsp/25 g/1 oz butter
1 cup/100 g/4 oz potatoes, peeled and diced
1 cup/100 g/4 oz carrots, scraped and thinly sliced
1 cup/100 g/4 oz onions, sliced
1–2 cloves garlic, chopped
1½ cups/100 g/4 oz cabbage, roughly shredded
2 cups/400 g/14 oz can butter beans, drained
1½ cups/400 g/14 oz can tomatoes, mashed, with juice
2½ cups/600 ml/1 pt hot beef stock
salt and freshly ground black pepper
4 slices crusty bread
Parmesan cheese

In Tuscany soup is often poured over a thick slice of bread in the bottom of the soup plate. It is a good way of using up the last slices of the loaf. You can toast the bread and rub it with a cut clove of garlic.

◆ Put the butter in a large pot and cook for 1 minute. Add the potatoes, carrots, onion and garlic, cover with vented cling wrap (plastic wrap) and cook for 8 minutes, stirring once.

◆ Add the remaining vegetables and pour on the beef stock. Cover and cook for 6 minutes, stirring once, until the potato and carrot are cooked. Season to taste.

◆ Lay a slice of crusty bread in each of 4 soup bowls. Pour on the soup and serve sprinkled liberally with Parmesan cheese.

VICHYSSOISE

SERVES 4 / SET: FULL

Ingredients

3 cups/350 g/12 oz potatoes, peeled and diced

1 onion, sliced

¾ cucumber

3 leeks, trimmed, washed and sliced

4 tbsp/50 g/2 oz butter

60 ml/4 tbsp water

2½ cups/600 ml/1 pt boiling chicken stock

salt and freshly ground black pepper

⅔ cup/150 ml/¼ pt single (cereal) cream

This soup is best served chilled on a hot summer's day.

◆ Put the potatoes in a bowl with the onion, two thirds of the cucumber, peeled and diced, the leeks, butter and water. Cover and cook for 10 minutes, stirring once.

◆ Pour on the boiling stock, cover and cook for 7 minutes, until the potatoes are soft, then blend in a liquidizer. Season, allow to cool and chill well.

◆ Serve cold with a swirl of cream and decorated with the remaining cucumber, thinly sliced.

Vichyssoise

POACHED EGGS ON SPINACH WITH HOLLANDAISE SAUCE

SERVES ·4
SET: FULL AND DEFROST

Ingredients

1 cup/225 g/8 oz frozen spinach, thawed and thoroughly drained

salt and freshly ground black pepper

4 eggs

Hollandaise Sauce (see page 51)

◆ Divide the spinach between 4 individual buttered ramekin dishes and cook on full power for 1½ minutes. Stir and season with salt and pepper.

◆ Break the eggs onto the spinach and prick the yolks gently with a cocktail stick to prevent them bursting. Cover the dishes with cling wrap (plastic wrap) and cook for 3 minutes on defrost power.

◆ Serve the Hollandaise sauce separately or pour over the eggs to serve.

THANKSGIVING SOUP

SERVES 4 / SET: FULL

Ingredients

15 ml/1 tbsp oil
1 onion, chopped
3 cups/350 g/12 oz squash (pumpkin), peeled, pips removed and diced
2 cups/250 g/8 oz carrots, chopped
2 potatoes, peeled and chopped
2½ cups/600 ml/1 pt boiling chicken stock
2 small courgettes (zucchini), thinly sliced
salt and freshly ground black pepper
parsley

◆ Put the oil in a pot and cook for 30 seconds. Add the onion, cover with vented cling wrap (plastic wrap) and cook for 2 minutes.

◆ Add the squash (pumpkin), carrots and potatoes and pour over the boiling stock. Cover and cook for 15 minutes, until the vegetables are soft, adding the courgettes (zucchini) 5 minutes before the end of cooking time.

◆ Keeping back most of the courgettes blend or partially blend the soup. Season to taste.

◆ Float the reserved courgettes on top and serve sprinkled with parsley.

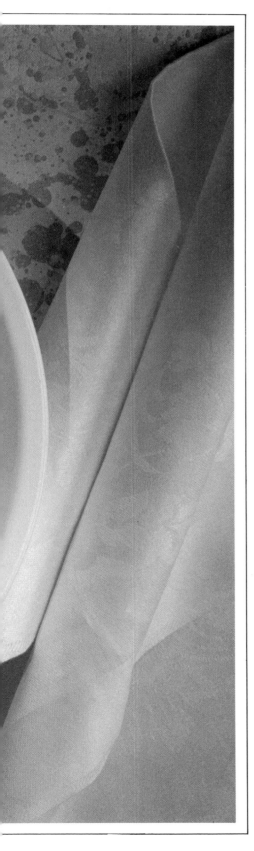

STUFFED CABBAGE LEAVES

SERVES 4
SET: FULL AND DEFROST

Ingredients

8 Savoy cabbage leaves
30 ml/2 tbsp water
2 tbsp/25 g/1 oz butter
1 onion, chopped
1 cup/175 g/6 oz cooked chicken or veal, chopped
1 cup/175 g/6 oz salami, derinded and chopped
30 ml/2 tbsp chopped fresh herbs
4 slices bread, crusts removed, soaked in milk, squeezed out and crumbled
salt and freshly ground black pepper
a little olive oil
TOMATO SAUCE
7 1/2 ml/1/2 tbsp oil
1/2 large onion, chopped
1/2 clove garlic, chopped
1 small carrot, chopped
1/2 stick (stack) celery, chopped
1 1/2 cups/200 g/7 oz can tomatoes, with juice
1/2 tbsp tomato purée (paste)
a few sprigs of basil
salt and freshly ground black pepper

◆ Choose even-sized cabbage leaves. Wash them well and trim off each stalk at its base. Put them in a boiling or roasting bag with the water, fasten the top loosely and cook for 4 minutes. Lay the leaves flat on a kitchen towel to absorb the excess water.

◆ Meanwhile make the sauce. Put the oil in a pot and cook for 30 seconds. Add the onion, garlic, carrot and celery and cook, covered with vented cling wrap (plastic wrap) for 4 minutes.

◆ Stir in the tomatoes and their juice, tomato purée (paste) and basil. Cover and cook for 8 minutes, stirring twice.

◆ Put the sauce in the liquidizer and blend until smooth, then season to taste.

◆ To make the filling for the cabbage leaves, put the butter in a pot and cook for 1 minute until melted. Stir in the onion, cover and cook for 3 minutes, until soft.

◆ Stir in the cooked chicken or veal, salami, herbs and breadcrumbs and season well, then divide the mixture between the cabbage leaves and roll up into parcels.

◆ Pack the cabbage parcels, join down, into a dish they just fit. Brush the tops with a little olive oil, cover the dish with vented cling wrap (plastic wrap) and cook on defrost setting for 8 minutes until hot through.

◆ Serve with the reheated tomato sauce.

CELERY SOUP

SERVES 4 / SET: FULL

Ingredients

3 tbsp/40 g/1 ½ oz butter
1 onion, chopped
½ head (bunch) celery, finely chopped
6 tbsp/40 g/1 ½ oz flour
1 ¼ cups/300 ml/½ pt milk
1 ¼ cups/300 ml/½ pt boiling chicken stock
salt and freshly ground black pepper
30 ml/2 tbsp cream
crispy bacon pieces

◆ Put the butter in a large pot and cook for 1 minute. Stir in the onion and celery, cover and cook for 4 minutes, until soft.

◆ Stir in the flour and cook for 1 minute. Stir in the milk and cook for 3 minutes, stirring every minute, until thick. Stir in the chicken stock and cook for a further 3 minutes. Season to taste.

◆ Pour into individual soup bowls, add a swirl of cream and sprinkle with crispy bacon pieces to serve.

SPINACH SOUP

SERVES 4 / SET: FULL

Ingredients

4 cups/1 kg/2 lb spinach
6 tbsp/80 g/3 oz butter
1 small onion, chopped
6 tbsp/40 g/1 ½ oz flour
1 ¼ cups/300 ml/½ pt milk
1 ¼ cups/300 ml/½ pt chicken stock
salt and freshly ground black pepper
2 egg yolks
30 ml/2 tbsp cream
2 slices white bread, cut into 1-cm/ ⅓-in dice

◆ Wash the spinach, discarding discoloured leaves and tough stalks. Pack it into a large pot, cover and cook for 6 minutes, turning once, until tender. Purée the spinach in a liquidizer.

◆ Put half the butter in the pot and cook for 1 minute until melted. Add the onion and cook for 1 minute. Stir in the flour and cook for 1 minute.

◆ Whisk in the milk and cook for 3 minutes, whisking every minute. Whisk again until the sauce is smooth.

◆ Stir in the spinach, pour on the chicken stock and stir well. Cook to heat through for 4 minutes. Season to taste.

◆ Whisk the egg yolks with the cream, stir into the soup and heat for 30 seconds.

◆ Ladle the soup into individual soup bowls and serve garnished with croûtons made by frying the diced bread on the hob in the remaining butter until golden.

VARIATION This soup can also be made with sorrel or young nettles, picked before the plants flower.

Spinach soup.

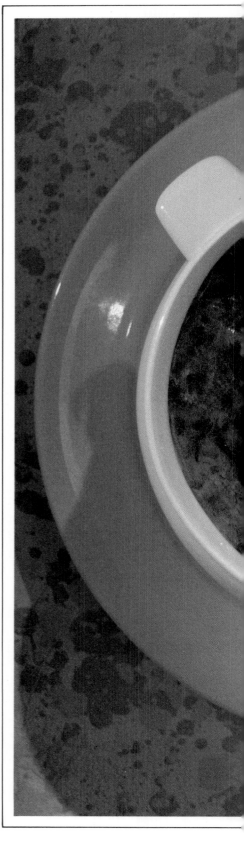

FRESH VEGETABLES/COOKING GUIDE

vegetables	quantity	minutes on full
globe artichokes	4	10 – 20
asparagus spears	1½ cups/225 g/8 oz	6 – 7
aubergines (eggplant), diced	2 cups/450 g/1 lb	5 – 6
beans, broad (fava, lima), French (green) or runner	2½ cups/450 g/1 lb	8 – 10
beetroot (beets), sliced	4 cups/450 g/1 lb	7 – 8
broccoli florets	6 cups/450 g/1 lb	4 – 5
Brussels sprouts	6 cups/450 g/1 lb	8 – 10
cabbage, shredded	6 cups/450 g/1 lb	7 – 10
carrots, sliced	2 cups/225 g/8 oz	7 – 10
cauliflower florets	6 cups/450 g/1 lb	10 – 11
celery	1 head	10 – 13
corn on the cob	1	3 – 5
courgettes (zucchini), sliced	4	7 – 10
Kohlraki	4 cups/450 g/1 lb	7 – 8
leeks, sliced	4 cups/450 g/1 lb	7 – 10
marrow (squash), sliced	4 cups/450 g/1 lb	8 – 10
mushrooms, whole	2½ cups/225 g/8 oz	5 – 6
okra	4 cups/450 g/1 lb	8 – 10
onions, sliced	2 cups/225 g/8 oz	5 – 7
parsnips, sliced	2 cups/225 g/8 oz	8 – 10
peas	4 cups/450 g/1 lb	7
potatoes, new	6 cups/450 g/1 lb	8 – 10
potatoes, jacket (baked)	2 large	8
potatoes, boiled	4 cups/450 g/1 lb	6 – 7
spinach	2 cups/450 g/1 lb	5
greens, chopped	6 cups/450 g/1 lb	7 – 9
swedes (rutabaga), sliced	3 cups/450 g/1 lb	6 – 7
tomatoes, sliced	1½ cups/450 g/1 lb	2 – 3
turnips, sliced	1½ cups/225 g/8 oz	6 – 7

FROZEN VEGETABLES/COOKING GUIDE

vegetables	quantity	minutes on full
asparagus spears	1½ cups/225 g/8 oz	6 – 7
beans, broad (fava), French (green) or runner	1½ cups/225 g/8 oz	7
broccoli spears	4 cups/225 g/8 oz	6 – 8
cabbage, chopped	3 cups/225 g/8 oz	6 – 7
carrots, sliced	2 cups/225 g/8 oz	6 – 7
cauliflower florets	4 cups/225 g/8 oz	4 – 6
sweetcorn (corn)	2 cups/225 g/8 oz	4 – 6
corn on the cob	1	4 – 5
courgettes (zucchini), sliced	2 cups/225 g/8 oz	4
peas	2 cups/225 g/8 oz	4
spinach, chopped	3 cups/225 g/8 oz	5
swedes (rutabaga), cubed	2 cups/225 g/8 oz	7
turnips, sliced	1½ cups/225 g/8 oz	8
vegetables, mixed	2 cups/225 g/8 oz	4 – 6

FRESH MEAT COOKING GUIDE

meat	minutes on full per 450 g/1 lb	standing minutes
bacon (ham) roast	12 – 14	10
bacon, rashers (slices) 4	4½	—
beef, boned roasts, rare	5 – 6	15 – 20
beef, boneless roast, medium	7 – 8	15 – 20
beef, boneless roast, well-done	8 – 9	15 – 20
beef, roasts with bone, rare	5 – 6	15 – 20
beef, roasts with bone, medium	6 – 7	15 – 20
beef, roasts with bone, well-done	8 – 9	15 – 20
beef, ground, 4 patties	10	5
chicken, whole roast	8 – 10	10 – 15
chicken, portions	6 – 8	10
lamb, boned roast	7 – 8	20
lamb, boned and rolled roast	9	20
lamb, roast with bone	6 – 7	20
lamb, crown roast	9 – 10	20
lamb chops	2	10
liver, ox (beef)	8	5
liver, lamb, calves'	7	5
pork, boned rolled roast	8 – 10	15
pork, roast with bone	8 – 9	15
poussin (Cornish rock hen), pigeon, pheasant, quail	5 – 7	5
sausages (links), 4	4	—
portions	15	10
turkey, whole roast	11	10 – 15

FROZEN MEAT DEFROSTING GUIDE

meat	minutes on low per 450 g/1 lb	standing minutes
beef, boned roasts	8 – 10	30
beef, roasts on bone	8 – 10	30
beef, minced (ground)	8 – 10	2
beef steak, cubed	6 – 8	5
hamburgers, two	2	2
hamburgers, four	4	2
chicken, whole	6 – 8	30
chicken portions	5	30
duck and duckling	5 – 7	30
kidney	6 – 9	5
lamb, boned roasts	5 – 6	30 – 45
lamb, with bone	8 – 10	30 – 45
lamb chops	8 – 10	15
liver	8 – 10	5
pork, boned roasts	7 – 8	30
pork roast with bone	7 – 8	45
poussin (Cornish rock hen), grouse, pigeon, pheasant	5 – 7	10
sausages (links)	5 – 6	5
turkey, whole	10 – 12	60
veal, boned rolled roast	5 – 6	30
veal, with bone	8 – 10	45
veal chops	8 – 10	30
veal, minced (ground)	8 – 10	5

FISH

Defrost and Cooking Guide

fish	*weight*	*defrost minutes*	*standing minutes*	*cooking in minutes on full*
bass	225 g/8 oz	5 – 6	15	5 – 6
bonito tuna steaks,	225 g/8 oz	10	15	—
bream, sea-bream	225 g/8 oz	—	15	10 – 12
cod fillets	225 g/8 oz	4 – 5	5	4 – 6
cod steaks	225 g/8 oz	5	5	6
crab claws	100 g/4 oz	5	5	2 – 3
crab, dressed (crab cakes)	100 g/4 oz	2	10	—
haddock fillets	100 g/4 oz	4 – 5	5	5 – 7
haddock steaks	100 g/4 oz	4 – 5	5	4 – 7
halibut steaks	100 g/4 oz	4 – 5	5	4 – 5
hake steaks	100 g/4 oz	4 – 5	5	4 – 6
kipper (kippered herrings)	100 g/4 oz	—	—	1 – 2
kipper (kippered herrings) fillets (boil-in-the-bag)	200 g/7 oz	3	5	3
mackerel	225 g/8 oz	6 – 8	8 – 10	4 – 5
mahi-mahi	225 g/8 oz	6 – 8	—	4 – 6
red and grey mullet	225 g/8 oz	6 – 8	8 – 10	4 – 6
mussels	225 g/8 oz	5	5	—
plaice (flounder) fillets	225 g/8 oz	4 – 5	5	4
prawns (small shrimp), cooked	225 g/8 oz	5	5	—
red salmon steaks	225 g/8 oz	5	5	4 – 5
scrod fillets	225 g/8 oz	4 – 5	30	4 – 5
scampi (king prawns), raw		5	5	4 – 6
scallops	225 g/8 oz	5	5	5 – 7
snapper	225 g/8 oz	6 – 8	8 – 10	5 – 7
sole	225 g/8 oz	5 – 6	8 – 10	4
trout	225 g/8 oz	6 – 8	8 – 10	7
yellowtail	225 g/8 oz	6 – 8	8 – 10	7

TIME AND SETTINGS FOR PASTA AND GRAINS

Although there are no real time savings in cooking rice and pasta in the microwave, it may be a more foolproof way of cooking as there is no risk of sticking to the pan. Standing is usually necessary to complete cooking.

Cooking times will vary according to the type of pasta. Fresh pasta needs microwaving for only 1 minute. It requires no standing time, but should just be drained and served immediately. Times for dried pasta and rice are given below.

PASTA AND GRAINS COOKING GUIDE PER 225 G/8 OZ

food	*boiling salted water to add*	*cooking in minutes on full*	*standing minutes*
long grain rice (1 generous cup)	3 cups/725 ml/1¼ pt	14	5
pudding (Carolina) rice (1 generous cup)	2½ cups/600 ml/1 pt		
American (converted) rice (2½ cups)	2½ cups/600 ml/ 1 pint	12	5
brown rice	3½ cups/900 ml/ 1½ pt	30	5
egg noodles & tagliatelle (fettucini) (6 cups)	4 cups/1 litre/1¾ pt with 2 tsp oil	6 – 8	2 – 3
spaghetti	4 cups/1 litre/1¾ pt with 2 tsp oil	12	5 – 10
pasta shells (2 cups) & shapes	4 cups/1 litre/1¾ pt with 2 tsp oil	12 – 14	5 – 10
macaroni (2 cups)	4 cups/1 litre/1¾ pt with 2 tsp oil	12 – 15	2 – 3
lasagne (6 cups)	4 cups/1 litre/1¾ pt with 2 tsp oil	9	2

CAKES, BREAD AND DESSERTS DEFROSTING GUIDE

product	*quantity*	*minutes on low*	*standing minutes*
bread, whole loaf	1 large	6 – 8	5 – 15
bread, whole loaf	1 small	4 – 6	10
bread, sliced loaf	1 large	6 – 8	10
bread, sliced loaf	1 small	4 – 6	5
bread slice	25 g/1 oz	10 – 15 secs	1 – 2
bread rolls, crumpets,	2	15 – 20 secs	1 – 2
scones (biscuits), etc	4	25 – 35	1 – 2
cakes, cream	2	45 – 60	10
	4	1¼	10
cakes, small	2	30 – 60	5
cupcakes	4	1¼ – 1¾	5
cakes, large:			
sponge (yellow) cake	450 g/1 lb	4	10
cheesecake	23 cm/9 in	3 – 4	20
dough, pizza and bread	450 g/1 lb	4	10
dough, shortcrust and puff	227 g/8 oz	4	20
dough, shortcrust and puff	397 g/14 oz	6	20
mousse (soufflé), small	1	30 secs	15
pie, fruit or cream	650 g/26 oz	5	10
trifle	1	1	15